# So we want our Children to Read?

50 fun strategies to make it happen

# Nancy Parato Goldhagen

Illustrated by Nanako Okubo
Lifelong Learning Systems, Inc.
Itasca, Illinois

Copyright June 1999

All rights reserved. No part of this book may be used or reproduced in any manner whatsoever without written permission of the publisher.

Printed in the United States of America
ISBN 0-9671548-0-4

# What people are saying

"When our son Stephen was four, we were both concerned with his academic abilities. We were contemplating holding him back a year. We then met Mrs. Goldhagen and her unique system of teaching reading. After only six months working with the Play & Read kit our son mastered all his phonics sounds (320 words) and 100 sight words. All this was accomplished with only 15 minutes a day. Stephen can now spell all (320) phonics words. He can read on the second grade level and his comprehension is excellent. This fall Steven will be entering first grade. We are grateful to Mrs. Goldhagen for introducing us to the Play & Read program."

-Tony and Phyllis Cimaglia

"Nancy Goldhagen's many years of teaching reading to young children have been highly successful. She has incorporated her techniques in the Play & Read kit. Teachers at the Science and Arts Academy highly endorse this excellent approach. It makes a child's first experience with reading one of enthusiasm and joy. I strongly endorse this reading program."

-Dr. Helene Bartz, Founder
Science and Arts Academy

"We were blessed to have Mrs. Goldhagen in our district. Her presentation of Play & Read was well received by the staff. Teachers raved about the responses that they received from their students. Children were taking an active part in this highly motivating program. Mrs. Goldhagen has enthusiasm that carries over to others. She is extremely knowledgeable and full of energy. We will need to solicit her help again in the future."

-Dr. Billy J. Mitchell, Superintendent
Pembroke Community Consolidated Schools
Hopkins Park, Illinois

Other products by Nancy Parato Goldhagen:

Play & Read: Matching, Making, Reading and Spelling (a phonics program)

Sight Words and Pictures (a whole language program)

Spoons on the Moon (a children's book)

A Snail in the Pail (a children's book)

More children's books to be announced.....

These products can be purchased by writing or calling:

Lifelong Learning Systems, Inc.
P.O. Box 186
Itasca, IL 60143
Phone: (630)773-2363
Fax: (630)773-0023
E-mail: Lifelong9@aol.com

# DEDICATION

To my daughters
Maria and Roseanne
whose passion for reading
has filled
my life with joy.

# Acknowledgements

This book would not have been possible without the support of my family. I am grateful to my husband, Richard, for his many years of patience and to my two babies, who inspired and "forced" me to create. Grown up now, they have assisted me in the typing and editing of the manuscript. A special thank you goes to all my students, too numerous to be mentioned by name, who have excelled and given me the incentive to write. Their parents' faith in my work has encouraged me through the years in this most challenging mission. Credit goes to my friends who have supported me year after year in the process of creating and finally publishing this book for children and parents.

# Foreword

I feel compelled to write this book because I have a vision and a mission to fulfill. At this moment as my pencil moves along, I see images of little people looking at me, their eyes wide open, sparkling with excitement. My students, I call them my children, have dreams and expectations. When we're together, everything we do is new and exciting for them. I can tell because we laugh a lot and we have so much fun. My children become happy readers; some develop a passion for books. All benefit one way or another after a short exposure to this system of reading. The youngest ones are so fresh and innocent, so easily amused by my silly games. All are so precious to me. And the proud parents are those who give me the privilege to teach, even for a short time, God's most awesome creation. I would like all children to have the opportunity to learn to read in a playful and joyful way, to be introduced to the pleasures of reading by a loving parent, caretaker or teacher.

Every child deserves a chance to be introduced to the wealth of knowledge gained through the written language. It should begin early, ideally in the warm and loving atmosphere of a home. There are experiences of joy and excitement I cannot keep to myself. I remember so vividly those early days when my two girls, at the age of four, began to read for everyone present, out loud, and refused to stop because the story was not yet over. Those were memorable and precious moments when I thought my heart was going to burst. I was smiling from ear to ear. In those days I had the urge to stand on the roof top or on a crowded street corner; I wanted to scream at the top of my lungs to let everyone know one simple fact- very young children can read, if we the adults will only teach them. In spite of my M.A. degree, I discovered this only after my babies were born.

I abandoned, for obvious reasons, the idea of a rooftop or a street corner. I must tell you though, that I still have that urge to shout at the top of my lungs in an attempt to share what I have learned. This book, in a sense, is my rooftop and my corner. My eyes fill with tears of joy. I am not ashamed to admit that my children have had this kind of impact on me.

When children are not introduced to reading in a playful way, whether at home or at school, instead of joy and excitement, there are tears, frustration, low grades, low self-esteem, and hours upon hours of struggle with homework. On a national level, early frustration with reading results in low standardized test scores, a high dropout rate and illiteracy. Parents come to the end of their rope, feeling helpless.

They want to give up and some do. I hear over and over again, "My child hates reading. I wish I had met you years ago."

I have a passion for reading and children. I have a mission to fulfill: anticipating, preventing failures, giving parents and teachers the fruits of twenty years of experience. It is my hope that these ideas and strategies will bring joy and excitement into your life as you introduce your child/students to the world of reading in a playful and positive way. Whether you have an eager child or a reluctant one, these pages are for you. And now, happy reading and have a warm and rewarding relationship with your child/students.

# TABLE OF CONTENTS

## Part I: A unique reading kit

1. A reading kit for everyone
2. The benefits of this reading kit

## Part II: How a child learns to read

1. Keep a positive attitude
2. Reading down to a science
3. Age appropriate
4. Time and Place
5. How much time
6. How fast can my child "grow" in reading?
7. The road to successful reading
8. How the brain perceives words
9. A child can read before he can speak

## Part III: Understanding the English Language

1. Phonics/Sight Words-understanding the difference: why phonics? why sight words?
2. List of 100 common words to be taught by sight

## Part IV: Strategies and how they work

1. What is a strategy?
2. List of 50 strategies: the key to playfulness
3. All 50 strategies, step by step

# A READING KIT FOR EVERYONE

1. EVERY PARENT
    a. Who desires to raise a bright child.
    b. Who has the inclination and enthusiasm for teaching.
    c. Whose time is valuable and who would not print, cut and paste hundreds of words.

2. A PRESCHOOLER who shows signs of wanting to learn to read.

3. A child in KINDERGARTEN who is anxious to gain independence in reading.

4. A FIRST GRADER who is being introduced to phonics/sight reading at school and would benefit from reinforcement at home.

5. A SECOND GRADER who has not mastered reading yet.

6. A THIRD GRADER who cannot read well and needs remedial work in reading and phonics in particular.

7. Children/adults studying ENGLISH AS A SECOND LANGUAGE

8. A child with LEARNING DISABILITIES who needs phonetic rules, and a clear reading system.

9. EVERY SCHOOL SYSTEM where reading in the lower grades is given top priority.
    a. in a classroom situation
    b. in one-on-one teaching
    c. in remedial reading
    d. in gifted programs

10. EVERY TEACHER who desires to be creative and successful in teaching reading.

11. EVERY LIBRARY with a lending system where educational games can be taken out.

# WHAT ARE THE BENEFITS OF THIS READING KIT?

1. To give a child the gift of reading, the greatest gift a parent can give, after love and affection.

2. To make the experience of learning to read at home or at school an enjoyable one.

3. To ensure that your child will have access to the number one tool for academic success.

4. To make your child an independent reader.

5. To build SELF ESTEEM. Early readers enjoy the distinction of being in the highest reading group.

6. To introduce reading at home in an atmosphere that does not include time limits, competition, pressure, restrictions, grades, frustration and possible failures, insuring that your child's experience will be a positive one.

7. To allow a young reader to read advanced books in his leisure time.

8. To prepare a child for the inevitable academic pressures that begin around fourth or fifth grade when many hours of reading are required.

9. To reduce the likelihood of the necessity of stressful parental involvement night after night in the painful process called "doing homework."

10. To give teacher and children the experience of learning to read with a step by step approach that is playful and joyful at the same time.

# KEEPING A POSITIVE ATTITUDE

1. Believe in your child's/students' innate ability to read.

2. Be joyful, playful, flexible.

3. Allow movement.

4. Observe your child/children so you will know what works.

5. Remember that there are no failures on learning to read. Each experience is a step forward in the learning process.

6. Praise and always reward your child/children with hugs, kisses, certificates, edible treats, or anything appropriate to your setting.

7. Create an atmosphere of success by filling the Progress Chart with stars, red dots, and stickers.

8. Give a written award every time your child/children learns to read a new set of words. Remember it is a big accomplishment.

9. Express joy in words: Excellent, good, great, super, wonderful. In action: Display joy with clapping, laughing, singing, etc.

10. Make no restrictions on the time or place for reading if possible.

11. Make your kit available to your child one set at a time.

12. Respect your child/children. When possible, give choices: now, later, here, there, this strategy or that one.

13. Share progress with family members. In a school setting, display students' progress chart for parents, teachers and principal to see.

14. Build memories by taking pictures, movies, etc.

15. Display your child's/students' progress chart so it can be seen.

# READING DOWN TO A SCIENCE

Reading is a natural process, like walking, talking, moving etc. All these activities are functions of the brain. When a child is given an opportunity to hear the spoken language, he learns to speak. Likewise, when a child is given the opportunity to see written language, he learns to read. However, learning to read should not be a hit and miss process. Teaching reading is a step-by-step activity that produces results. It is very much like gardening. A bean seed will sprout and grow into a green bean plant. Tender plants need, at the beginning, the daily care of water and sunshine. Careful tending and "nurturing" continues until a plant develops deep roots. Without care a young plant will surely die. This analogy applies to children and reading.

Every child has an innate ability to read and every adult has the ability to teach reading. However, teaching reading is not natural but an art to be acquired. This book is a result of 20 years of experience. Now parents/teachers don't need to re-invent the wheel. By using these fun-filled strategies, you will succeed at teaching your child/students to read. Through research and first hand observation I have seen proof that teaching reading is indeed a science.


Note: Children with learning disabilities have responded well to our unique reading system.

# AGE APPROPRIATE

Parents ask me "When is the right time to begin to teach my child to read?" Children are ready to begin anytime. Parents often are not. The right time is any time you the parent feel comfortable doing so. I have known many children who have "pushed" the parents to teach them to read. Some five-year-olds are more eager than others to begin learning to read. But all children should be introduced to reading in a loving atmosphere before starting school.

I may be criticized for suggesting that written words could be introduced at the age of two. The question is, what is age appropriate? Learning happens in a natural way. Scientists are discovering more and more the amazing minds of infants. Babies have an innate ability to respond to language, physics, math, and emotions. They even remember sequences! My first child, an early talker, used to look up every time an airplane passed by. We live close to O'Hare airport in Chicago. I used to tell her, "Grandma will be coming to visit us-she'll be coming in an airplane." So I decided to purchase a globe to show her where Grandma was coming from. She was only 16 months old. Her deep interest in countries led me to buy a U.S. puzzle. She was only two when she could read all the names of the states and put the pieces together in three minutes.

A word of caution is appropriate here. There is a fine line between "pushing" and "stifling." Careful observation of your child's responses will tell you when to stop. Nature cannot be hurried. My first child, an early talker, spoke her first clear word at three months. I was concerned when my second baby was two years old and was not talking yet! But there was nothing wrong with her and both girls displayed the same natural ability in the area of reading. Whether one begins at five or at two or even before, the strategy and duration should be appropriate for your child.

## TIME AND PLACE

Reading just happens. It happens just like talking happens. When we want to say something to our baby, we do without hesitation. We're not concerned that the baby is hearing a language he has never heard before. We think it is natural and we are right. Reading should happen in the same natural way, without much concern that the written language is something your child has never seen before. Let me illustrate what I mean. Since there are printed words everywhere, I took the opportunity for reading by pausing and reading for my children. The sign "car wash" at a gas station caught my attention as I was driving, so rather than making a right turn at the end of the street, I made a right turn at the gas station, drove slowly by the sign, and showed my child the "car wash" sign. From that time on she could read "car wash" every time she saw those words.

## HOW MUCH TIME?

"How long should I work with my child?" is one of the questions most often asked. The answer depends on the child, the parents and the circumstances. Some parents of successful readers have reported to me that they have spent no more than ten minutes per day. These are parents who both work full time. Ten minutes sounds just right; however, these ten minutes can be spread one minute here and one minute there. The following pages will give you strategies to make this happen. As a parent, you will want to "catch the moment" and read when the occasion arises: in the house, on the road, at the store, etc. When these moments occur they can add up to the ten minutes necessary for success. You need not feel "guilty" about not having a set time and place for reading. Observing a child's desire to continue or stop is crucial; in fact, usually it is wise to stop even before he says stop. However, there will be times when the fun cannot and should not be stopped. These will be memorable times when there's fun, laughter and even silliness. Enjoy the moment and celebrate!

# HOW FAST CAN MY CHILD "GROW" IN READING?

Even a very young child can "grow" two words per day. On day one after you have played Strategy #1, "Let's Make a Train" and Strategy #3, "Hide and Seek," (as you will see in the following pages) your child will point to two of his "favorite" words e.g. mommy and daddy. Tomorrow you will focus on two more words. On the third day, review the four words already mastered and add two more, e.g. eggs. Continue to let your child "grow" two words per day.

| mommy | daddy |
|---|---|
| boy | ice cream |

In so doing you will give your child a taste of success. The Play & Read Phonics can be handled the same way. After matching the "oo" words have your child focus on zoo and school, then add moon and food. There are 16 words. In less than two weeks your child will have mastered all 16 words. The next set on the progress chart is the "ar" sound. Allow your child to master this sound in two weeks at most. By the third sound, the "all" words, your child is beginning to understand the concept of reading. Now he can go through all 16 words in five days or a week. Most children "grow" one set of phonics (16 words) and one set of 10 sight words per week. You and your child may go through all 320 words in the phonics kit in 20 weeks and all sight words, 100 of them in 10 weeks. Some children need more time and should not be "pushed," but children who are able to grow faster should not be "stifled" either. You the parent (mom or dad) need to make goals for yourself. A growth of about two phonics words and two sight words per day is just about right. Just think-in less than a year your child will be able to read easy books. When introduced to all the strategies described in this book, some bright and eager children are able to go from a first grade reading level, to a second, third, fourth and fifth grade reading level in about six months. The video provided in the Play & Read kit shows two students reading a 5th grade reading book. Both had just completed kindergarten and had been my students for less than a year. Obviously not all students grow this fast. However, all kindergarten-age children who go through this reading program are at least one year ahead of their peers by the time they reach first grade.

# THE ROAD TO SUCCESSFUL READING

How do children learn to read? How does the mind perceive words? Reading by sight is one method; reading by phonics is another. These two methods complement each other and should be taught simultaneously. Neither method is sufficient in itself.

Some words are strictly "sight words." The words laugh and eye, for instance, cannot be explained phonetically. It would be a mistake to explain that sometimes "gh" makes the "f" sound. Why burden and confuse a child with more rules? Since the words laugh and eye are unique, they are best learned through strategies such as flashing and hide and seek. Some words can be learned through a combination of sight and phonics. The word shoes for example, can be explained phonetically only in part.

Phonics will strengthen sight learning and vice versa. Phonics will be a life-long tool to be used with new and unknown words. Some words, however, are not phonetic and must be learned as a unit.

Phonics through Play & Read has been designed to provide fun and enjoyment for both parent and child/teacher and children. Sight words when introduced in a playful way, will add enjoyment to _process_ of reading. Remember that the child's progress in learning sight words and phonics is important, but only as a means to an end. The ultimate goal is to instill in the child a strong desire to read. If the child is to love reading, his first experiences with learning to read must be positive. Therefore it is crucial that parents and teachers be as creative and playful as possible.

Through my experience with children, I have found the strategies in this booklet to be the most effective.

# HOW THE BRAIN PERCEIVES WORDS

Some ways in which the brain receives the message "apple."

#1    | apple |    the <u>real</u> apple, your child will see.

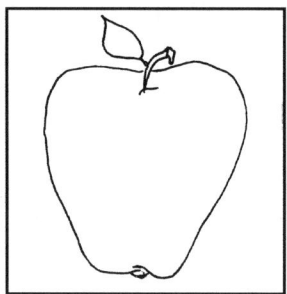

#2    | apple |    the <u>real</u> apple your child will touch.

#3    | apple |    the <u>picture</u> of an apple your child will see.

#4 | apple | the spoken word apple, your child will hear.

$$\boxed{\text{apple}}$$

#5 | apple | the written word apple, your child will see.

$$\boxed{\text{apple}}$$

#6 | apple | the written-spoken word apple, your child will see and hear.

$$\boxed{\text{apple}}$$

# A CHILD CAN READ BEFORE HE CAN SPEAK

Parents delight in the process of showing babies a beautiful red apple. They are convinced that the baby is learning the names of things. They are ecstatic when they ask the baby to point to "apple" and the baby is able to do so. A common activity between a child and parent is parents asking questions such as these:

> Where is daddy?
> Where is mommy?
> Where is the apple?
> Where is your teddy bear?

The baby then points to these objects or people and the parents are overjoyed. Parents perform quite well on the "message"

> #1 real apple-see
> #2 real apple-touch
> #3 picture apple-see
> #4 spoken word apple-hear

This is where most parents stop. The written-spoken word is not presented to the child until kindergarten or first grade. Many parents wait until the child is able to say the word apple. The thinking is that if the baby cannot speak, how can he possibly read?

The fact is, that the baby CAN read before he can speak! The brain "sees" and "hears." My second child, who could not speak until she was two, correctly and consistently pointed to words long before she turned two.

The baby can point to words before he can say them. Pointing to words is reading. Suppose you flash these words.

| mommy | daddy | milk | apple |

Then ask your child to point to mommy; you will see that he can.

# PHONICS/SIGHT WORDS:
## UNDERSTANDING THE DIFFERENCE

Why Phonics?

While English is not a completely phonetic language, it is crucial for parents to provide groups of words with similar sounds. The phonics component of any reading program should teach beginning sounds, e.g. moon vs. room, ending sounds e.g. boot vs. boom and blends e.g. scoop, groom etc. These words are sounded out. However, as we shall see, not all words should be read by this method. For instance, if we taught long words like strawberries by sound, we would have to say s....t...r...a...w...b...e...r...r...i...e...s ... It is clear that we don't have to sound out every letter in the word to make our students learn to read that word. Reading a word like baby could become a tedious task if we were to say this is b...a...b...y. If you use this method your child will most likely run away to play with his toys. This process is too long and too tedious.

Remember: English is not totally phonetic. Many words will be taught as sight words; others will be taught as phonics.

A clear and comprehensive phonics program is a crucial part of any reading system. The Play & Read: matching, making, reading, spelling kit was designed to make the process of reading fun and playful. This is part of the kit, one of 20 boards introducing the sound of oo as in zoo. It can be purchased by contacting the publisher of this book.

| scoop | noon | boot | zoom |
|---|---|---|---|
| groom | boom | room | pool |
| roof | moon | broom | spoon |
| zoo | school | food | gloom |

Why Sight words?

While phonics will teach your child beginning and ending sounds, blends and groups of similar sounds, some words will not follow the rules. It is unnecessary, in fact, a burden to your child to memorize the rules. Your child will have learned that **ea** will say,

| | |
|---|---|
| meat | neat |
| seat | steam |
| heat | eat |
| cream | clean |
| team | seat |
| dream | neat |

The following ea words will not follow the eat and meat sound. These words are best learned as sight words, which means as a unit. The train and flash strategies work well for these words.

| | |
|---|---|
| wear | learn |
| pear | head |
| heart | steak |
| early | learn |
| ready | bread |
| heavy | earn |

# 100 Common Words to be Taught by Sight

1. apple
2. baby
3. ball
4. banana
5. beans
6. bird
7. black
8. blue
9. boat
10. bones
11. boy
12. bread
13. broccoli
14. brother
15. brown
16. bus
17. butter
18. cabbage
19. cat
20. cake
21. carrot
22. chicken
23. children
24. closet
25. corn
26. cup
27. daddy
28. danger
29. dog
30. doll
31. door
32. dress
33. ear
34. eggs
35. elephant
36. enter
37. exit
38. eye
39. finger
40. fish
41. flower
42. girl
43. grapes
44. green
45. hair
46. hand
47. hat
48. head
49. heart
50. horse
51. hospital
52. ice cream
53. jelly
54. kitchen
55. knee
56. leg
57. lemon
58. lobster
59. man
60. meat
61. milk
62. mommy
63. monkey
64. nose
65. office
66. onions
67. orange
68. pajamas
69. pear
70. plate
71. plums
72. police
73. potato
74. purple
75. queen
76. rabbit
77. red
78. shoes
79. shrimp
80. sister
81. spinach
82. steak
83. stomach
84. store
85. strawberries
86. table
87. toes
88. tomato
89. tongue
90. turkey
91. umbrella
92. violin
93. wagon
94. walk
95. water
96. white
97. window
98. xylophone
99. yellow
100. zebra

# WHAT IS A STRATEGY?

In this book, it is an umbrella word to describe:

      1. material used
      2. games to be played
      3. places to go
      4. children's involvement
      5. teachers'/parents' approach
      6. home vs. school setting
      7. ideas old and new
      8. time and place etc.
      9. activities

In other words, strategies are the many possible ways to introduce the written language. They all lead to the ultimate goal: an independent and happy reader. Parents and teachers will select those strategies appropriate to their situation.

Remember: you need not feel overwhelmed when faced with these 50 strategies. Select those you and your child/children like most. All my children (students) are very enthusiastic when I announce "let's make a train."


The following are strategies I have used with my own children as well as my students. They have proven to be very effective.

# STRATEGIES: THE KEY TO PLAYFULNESS

1. Matching words to pictures
2. Let's make a train
3. Hide and seek
4. See four, give me one
5. Flashing
6. Your favorite word
7. Songs: Twinkle, Twinkle Little Star
8. Reading on the road
9. Street signs
10. Matching street signs to street signs
11. Matching words to street signs
12. Matching words to numbers
13. Matching words to colors
14. Matching words to animals
15. Matching words to countries
16. Matching states to states
17. U.S. puzzle
18. Finding countries in each continent
19. The globe
20. The solar system
21. Opposites
22. Poetry
23. Songs
24. Play store
25. Let's go shopping.
26. Electric board
27. Making sentences from known words
28. Flash and see all b words
29. Making stacks: all a words, b words, c words etc.
30. Beginning sound: each on one page
31. Silly b words
32. Body parts: cover body, point to body part
33. Label furniture
34. Pin words on cork board
35. Point to calendar
36. Names of family members

37. Names of famous people
38. Breakfast time
39. Grocery list on the refrigerator
40. Restaurant: napkin
41. Pencil and paper always
42. Circles and lines in a story
43. Advanced reading
44. Read notes-find a treat
45. Egg hunt - read a note - get a clue
46. Parents reading to children
47. Make up stories
48. Action words
49. Books on shelves
50. Notes in the lunch box



Remember: Ten to fifteen minutes per day is sufficient time for success.

# THE MAGIC OF MATCHING

The matching strategy is so powerful that it is nothing short of "magic"! You will use it over and over again.

Why so much matching? It "forces" the young learner to look at and focus upon the word again and again in an attempt to find its match. The word becomes a "unit" in his mind. It is like taking a photograph of that word. Show your child "apple" over and over again. What will happen? The word apple will appear in his brain again and again. The image is already there; it can reappear any time.

Remember: A child's self esteem must be nurtured. In every situation, whether one-on-one or with two or more children, making the child feel successful is crucial. For instance, one-on-one, asking your child to point to all his favorite words rather than requiring him to read all the words you have laid out, is setting him up for success. With two or more children, if one child can read more words than the other, and you want each child to read 10 out of 20 words, ask the child who knows less to first select ten of his favorite words. The remaining words will be read by the second child whom we know can do it. This will set everyone up for success.

We begin with food, one of the most important things in a child's life. We show how words are related to what he eats and enjoys.

# #1 Matching words to pictures

These 20 colorful pictures are useful for your 3, 4 or 5 year old child. Display all 20 pictures on the floor or on the table in a semicircle shape. Give your child one word at a time, read it to him (he may know one of the words and volunteer to read it for you) then ask him to match it to the picture. When all words are matched under a picture, have your child pick them up one by one. Say, "Give me the word banana," take it from him and repeat the process until all words have been picked up. Then ask your child to pick up all the pictures as well. It would be wise to make a collection of pictures. Newspaper ads will provide an abundance of colorful pictures, especially in the area of foods. They can be cut out, and if laminated, passed on to younger children.

# #2 Let's make a train

When talking to your child, you will always call this activity "Let's make a train." It is actually a matching activity that will give your child sure success. Line up 10 red words (different from each other) on the floor. Later, it can be done on a table. Give your child one blue word at a time, read it for him and ask him to go find its match and place it on top of the red card. The length (10, 20 or more) of the train depends on the child's interest; it will grow according to a child's progress. Success depends on playfulness. Ask your child to put one foot on one side and one on the other. Pretend to be a conductor. While searching for the word, your young child may make a train sound - choo, choo,.... Some children prefer to walk on the side of the "train." After all the red cards have been covered, ask your child to collect all the blue words. Now ask him to give you all his favorite words. Each time the train game is played, his reading vocabulary will increase. It is not unusual for a child to learn 10 or more words per week.

## Matching: 2 students/friends (non-competitive)

You have already prepared a train of twenty red words. Each child will come to you for a blue word which you will read and he will match. Continue until all twenty blue words have been placed on top of red words.

Matching: 2 students/friends (competitive)

You have already prepared a train with twenty red words. This time the children will not come to you. Each child has a chair with 10 blue words placed on it. Now each student will take one word at a time, read it or have the teacher read it for him, then go to the train and find its match. When the chair has no more words, the child can sit. Who will sit first?

## Matching : 4 students (non-competitive)

There are 40 red words on the floor or the table. You, the teacher, will hold all the blue words. Read a word and give it to one child. He will match it and return for another one. All four students will match about 10 words.

Matching: 4 students (competitive)

You have already prepared a train of 40 red words on the table. Each child has a chair with 10 blue words on it. Each child takes one word at a time, reads it or has the teacher read it for him, then finds its match. He then returns to his chair and continues the process until all his 10 words have been matched. When the chair is free of words, the child can sit. Who will sit first?

Matching: all students (non-competitive)

This is for a preschool or kindergarten setting in which you have 20 students or more. You have already prepared a train of 10 red words on the floor. Choose 10 of your students and give each one a blue card to be matched. The other students will sit and watch. When they have matched all the words, collect all the blue words and do the same with the other half of the class. The next day, form a train of 20 red words so that all students can be involved. Perhaps the students can form a line to receive a blue word which you will read for them. After the word has been matched, each student will sit. Two volunteers will collect all the blue words; two more will pick up all the red words.

Matching: all students (competitive)

The children have practiced matching words for a few days. Now it is time to compete. Divide the children into two teams so that no one child will feel embarrassed for finishing second nor receive the entire credit for winning. The teamwork will give students a sense of camaraderie. Twenty words are on the floor. One blue word is on each desk. Two children, one from each group, are given the OK to stand up and match their words. When a child finds the match, he quickly sits down to allow another child from his team to get up and match. The team that finishes first wins.

Reading: one child

After all 10, 20 or 30 words have been matched, and the blue words collected, it is time to read. There are three ways your child can read for you:
1. Ask, "Where is your favorite word?" Have your child turn over each word he can read.
2. Your child may enjoy more movement, in which case he will point to a word, read it, wait for you to say OK, then take it to a chair and return for more.
3. The reading can be done by flashing. Hold all the cards and let your child read each one. The words he reads go upside down on the table; the words he does not read are read by you and placed in the back of the stack.

It is not unusual for a child to learn 10 new words per week. Some children learn even faster.

Reading: Two students/friends (non-competitive)

There are 10, 20 or 30 red words on the table. In turn each child will point to a word he knows, read it, and wait for the teacher to say OK. Then the child will turn over the word or take it to his chair.

These activities work well when both children are on the same reading level. In a classroom situation the teacher can call on two volunteers who seem to be equally prepared.

Reading: 2 students/friends (competitive)

After children have matched and have collected the blue words, 20 red words remain. Now each child will point to a word he knows, say the word, and wait for the teacher to say "O.K.," He will then take the word to his chair, and return for more. The children will read as quickly as they can. When all the words are gone, the teacher will count. Who is the winner? What happens if there are some words neither child can read? You will flash them again (see strategy #5). Line up the words again and let the children continue. The competitive element works well when both children are on the same level. Two children whose parents have purchased the 100 words can receive a star sticker on each word they know. When both children know the words there can be 2 tables; each table has as many as 30 words. Now each child will point, read, and wait for the teacher to say OK, then he will take that word to the chair or turn it over. If there are some words your child cannot read, you will flash them, mix the words, put them on the table, and let the child continue.

Reading: Four students/friends (non-competitive)

After all 10, 20, 30, or 40 words have been matched, and the blue words collected, what remains are the red words. Now the four students will point, say the words, hear "OK," and take the words to their chairs. In a competitive situation, the teacher will count the cards on each chair. Who is the winner? The student with the most words on his chair wins.

Reading:  Four students/friends (competitive)

Each student has 20 words in front of him. The teacher will move from child #1 to child #4.  Each child will point to a word he knows, say the word, wait for the teacher to say OK, and take that word to his chair.  Suppose a student reads a word incorrectly. The teacher will say, "almost," read the word for the student, then move on to another child. What if there are some words that none of the children can read? The teacher will flash the words, spread them on the table and move on. It is very important to give each child an equal number of turns.  The child who turns over all of his cards first wins.  While this activity is appropriate for a classroom situation, four parents can get together on a weekly basis and have their children play this game.

Reading: all students (non-competitive)

Students have been involved in the "Let's Make a Train" strategy. They have had fun matching blue words to red words. Two volunteers have collected all the blue words. What remains on the floor are 10, 20 or 30 words. At first, it would be wise to ask for a volunteer to choose his favorite word. Allow children to volunteer one by one. Your student will pick up a word, read it, and hand it to you. It is clear at this point that many students can read several words. To reinforce reading, do the flashing by holding all the cards and letting the class read each word. If the students read the word, it goes on a desk. If not, you will read it and put the word in the back of the stack. This activity is not only for a classroom situation, but also for a group of mothers who wish to get together and have their children play this game. It is important to make all children feel like winners.

Reading: all students (competitive)

Make a train of 50 red words. Choose five students to demonstrate the game to the rest of the class. In turn, each student will point to a word he knows, read it, hear "OK," and take it back to his desk. If a student cannot read any of the words, or reads his word incorrectly, he sits down and waits for his next turn. At the end, see who has the most words. When the game has been demonstrated, you can play with as many students as you wish.

Reading: Team A & B (competitive)

Divide the children into two teams, A and B. Have the children in team A sit on one side of the room and the children on team B sit on the other. Hold a stack of 50 words in your hand. The first child on team A will read the first word, then the first child on team B will read the second word. The second child on team A will read the third word, etc.... When the children read the words, place the cards face down. Make separate stacks of cards for teams A and B. If a child cannot read a word, you read it to the class and put it in the back of the stack. When all the words have been read, count the cards in each stack. The team with the most cards wins.

Reading: Team A & B (competitive)

A relay race is another way to generate enthusiasm. Prepare a train of 50 words on the floor or on a long table in the front of the classroom. Two students, one from each team, will simultaneously be ready to point, read, hear OK from the teacher, take the word to their desks and quickly sit down. Another student will quickly get up, read the word and allow the next student to get up. A student cannot get up unless the previous student has reached his chair. When all 50 cards have been picked up, the teacher will collect the words from each team, count them and announce the winner team. The goal for this activity is to encourage camaraderie, generate fun, and ultimately to teach reading.

# #3 Hide and seek

Very young children love this game. You can display 4 different words.

| apple | ice cream |

| milk | eggs |

Say to your child, "We're going to play hide and seek." Now lift one of the words and say "This is ice cream. Close your eyes, turn your head, don't look." Now change the position of the card.

| apple | milk |

| ice cream | eggs |

Now say, "O.K. Find ice cream." Your child will point to ice cream. If he/she doesn't, you say "You found _____." Then point to ice cream yourself and say "This is ice cream." Say to your child, "Let's do this again. Close your eyes, etc...." Make sure to change the position of ice cream.

| ice cream | eggs |
|---|---|
| milk | apple |

Repeat the game with all the words. At the end of this session, which will last no more than 2 minutes, your child will have learned 4 words.

Remember: Establishing a routine, perhaps working together every day after breakfast is advantageous, but not always possible. It is not advisable to maintain a routine at the cost of the child's comfort. The positive mood of parent and child is far more important.

# #4 See four, give me one

Display four different words. Fish, chicken, eggs and milk would be good choices, as they have different beginning sounds.

Say, "Give me fish." Suppose your child gives you eggs rather than fish. Then your reply should be, "That's eggs; here is fish." Continue by asking for a word other than fish or eggs. If the answer is correct, take fish and replace it with another word, e.g. orange.

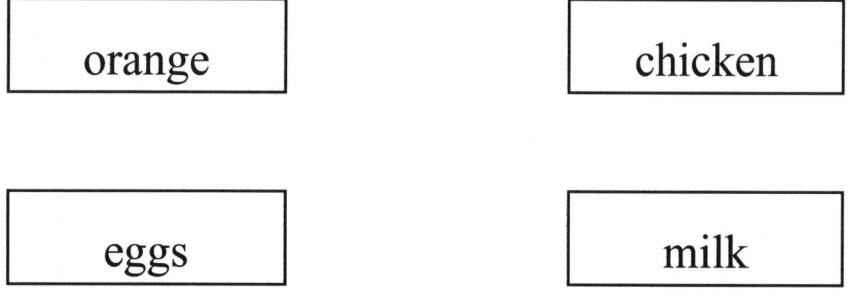

Continue the process until all (10 at first) words have been displayed. At first avoid displaying words with the same beginning sound, such as bread and beans. It is just as important to avoid words with similar beginning letters like b and d. These two symbols are very much alike and confuse most children. For example, do not show "boy" and "dog" at the same time until your child has mastered beginning sounds.

# #5 Flashing

Hold 10 words in your hand. Have your child face you. Say each word clearly and with expression, then place the cards on the table face down. Choose interesting words regardless of length or "difficulty." For instance, the word strawberries may have a special attraction for your child. Flash the words quickly so your child will not lose interest.

These are the words I find to be most effective:

| | |
|---|---|
| mommy | milk |
| daddy | eye |
| boy | ice cream |
| girls | strawberries |
| eggs | apple |

But you may decide to begin with 10 of the food words selected from the list below:

| | |
|---|---|
| apple | grapes |
| banana | ice cream |
| broccoli | lemon |
| butter | meat |
| cake | milk |
| carrot | onions |

| | |
|---|---|
| chicken | orange |
| corn | pear |
| eggs | strawberries |
| fish | tomato |

Your first 10 words should have different beginning sounds. For instance, cake and carrot, meat and milk, banana and butter should not be together in the first set. If food words are your choice, the following words would be appropriate:

| | |
|---|---|
| apple | grapes |
| banana | ice cream |
| eggs | fish |
| milk | strawberries |
| orange | lemon |

Remember:  The goal is for every child/student to be able to read all 100 words as the parent/teacher flashes them quickly.

# #6 Your favorite word

After "Hide and seek," "See four, give me one," and "Flashing," it is important to display all the words you have been working with. Say to your child, "This (lift it) is my favorite word. What is yours?" He/she will point to all the words he can read. Attach a star sticker to the upper right corner of every flash card he knows. It is time for you and your child to celebrate the first step toward a successful reading experience.

What happens after your child has successfully read 10 words? He is now ready to read 10 more words. Remember to be selective: choose words with different beginning sounds as well as those you think will appeal to him.

Remember: The principle of continuity. Ten or fifteen minutes each day is more advisable than one hour one time per week.

# #7 Songs: Twinkle, Twinkle Little Star

Apply what your child knows by memory to the printed word. Small children like to sing "Twinkle, Twinkle Little Star," but they have never seen the written form. When we point to every word and sing, children make an astounding discovery. They think, "Oh, that is what Twinkle looks like...."

> Twinkle, twinkle little star,
> how I wonder what you are.
> Up above the world so high
> like a diamond in the sky.
> Twinkle, twinkle little star,
> How I wonder what you are!

Point to each word and sing. Point to the word twinkle, then say, "This is twinkle. Find another twinkle in the song. At first your child will need a little help. Repeat the process with other words: little, star, etc. Make one flash card for each word in the song. Give one word to your child and say, "This is wonder, find wonder." Continue until all words have been found. Print each sentence on a strip of paper with red marker. Print individual words in green.

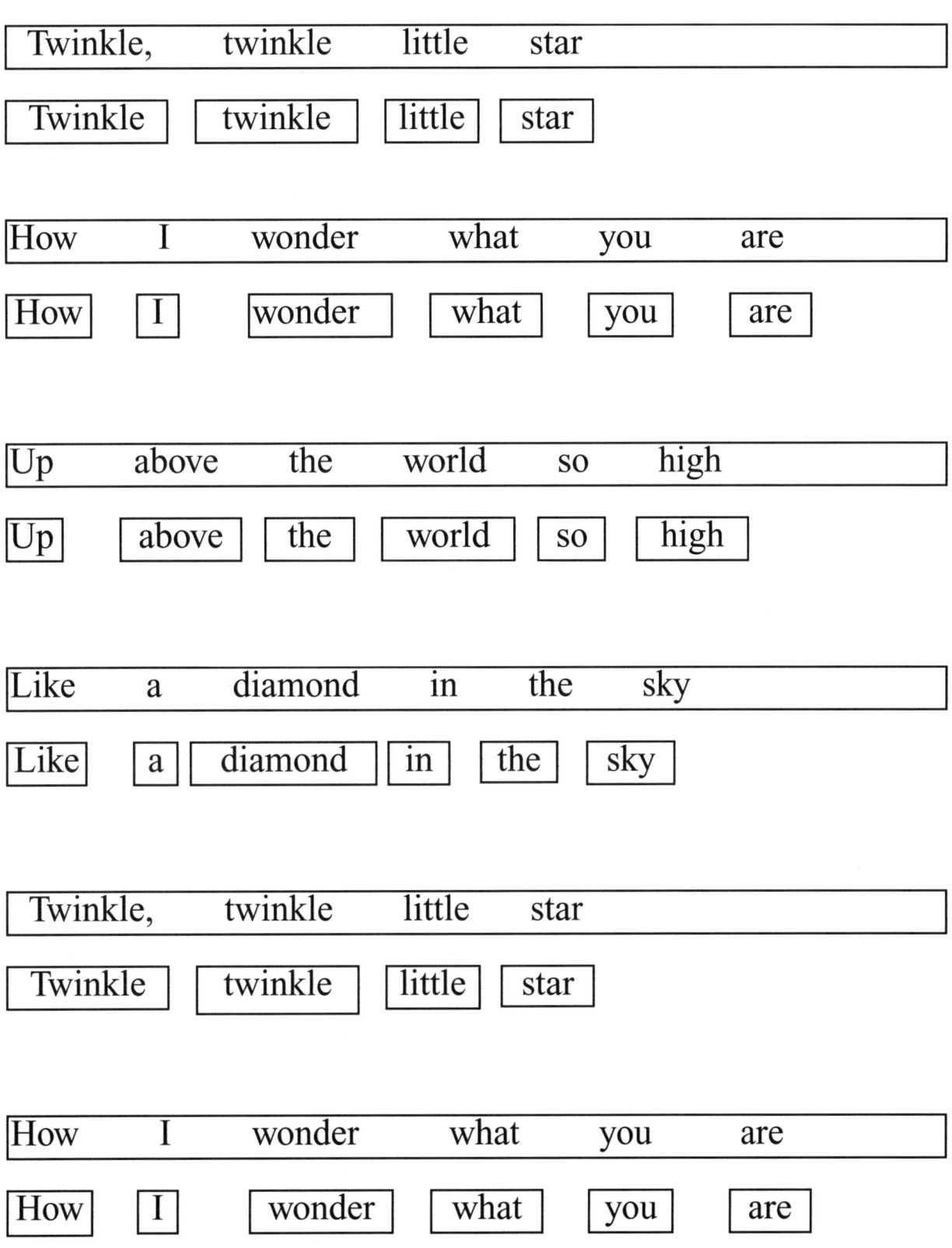

Let your child find each word to match the words in the sentence. Sing again; tell your child to follow the pencil pointing to each word. Your child will have a tendency to move faster than the pencil. Say, "Whoops! Wait for my pencil." You will soon discover that your child is singing by reading rather than by memory.

# #8 Reading on the road

There is so much to read as you travel! Even a short trip to the grocery store will provide reading material. Names of stores and restaurants are visible. Your child may see a police car, an ambulance, trucks with familiar words on them, e.g. Fruits & Vegetables. Street signs are everywhere. The words "car wash" can be seen at gas stations. Your task of pointing out words to your child on the road will not last very long. You will soon see that it is the young reader who will read all the signs. If it becomes a habit, it can be so much fun!

# #9 Street signs

Purchase street signs flash cards. Flash them. Display them around the house. Attach them to a cork board. Read them as you pass by. Ask your child to find the words "Stop," "Danger," etc....

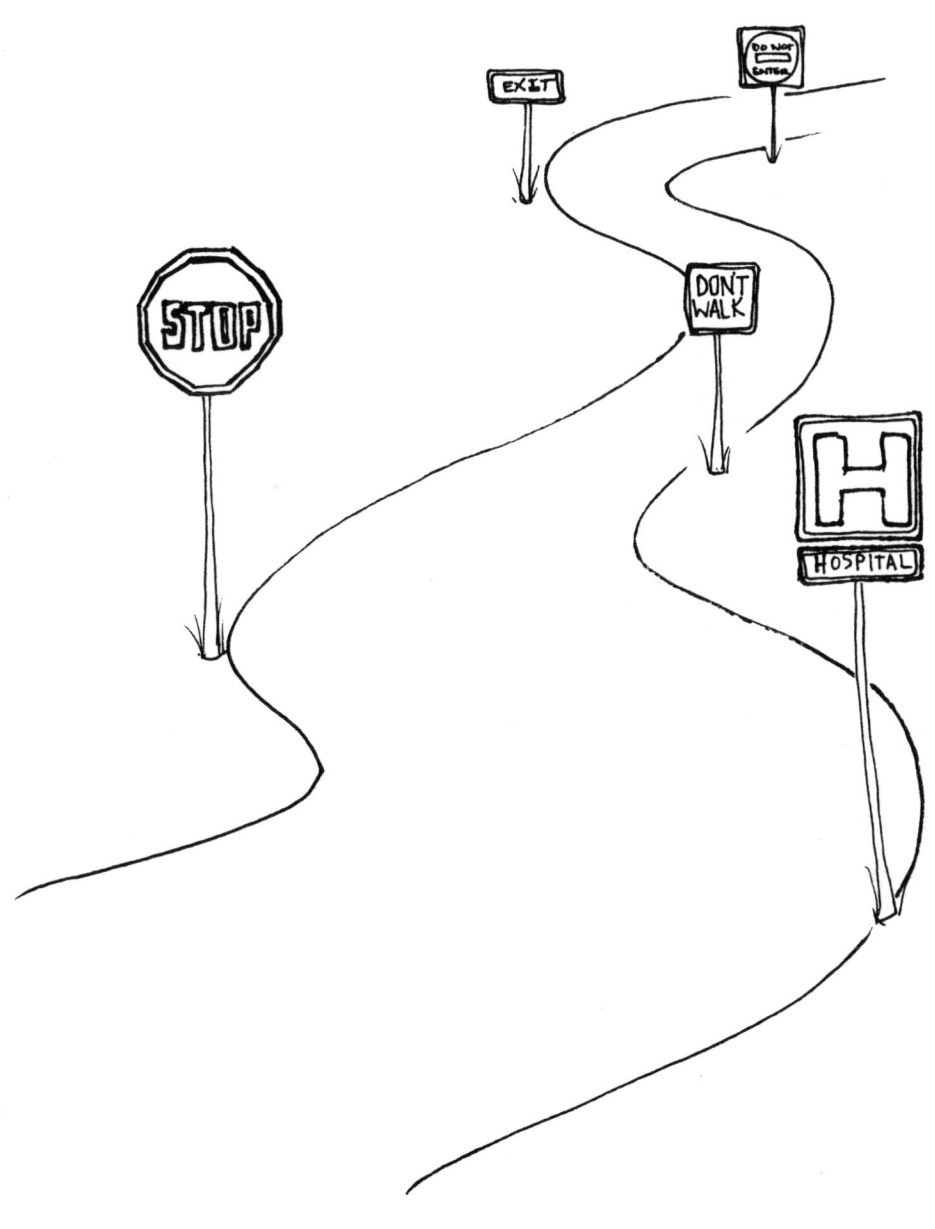

## #10 Matching street signs to street signs

The package of street sign cards you purchase may include a large and small version of street sign pictures. Have your child match the small to the large version of the same street signs, one large and one small. Ask your child to make two rows. Each sign will have its match.

## #11 Matching words to street signs

Create street signs flash cards by printing all the words on index cards with magic markers. Display the street signs on the floor or on the table. Read each index card and say, "This says 'danger.' Go find the sign that says 'danger.'" Continue the process until all words have been matched to street signs.

## #12 Matching words to numbers

Write the numbers 1 to 10 on a set of index cards. Write their corresponding words on another set of 10 index cards. Display the numbers vertically or horizontally, then give your child one word at a time, read it, and help him or her find the matching number.

| | |
|---|---|
| 1 | one |
| 2 | two |
| 3 | three |
| 4 | four |
| 5 | five |
| 6 | six |
| 7 | seven |
| 8 | eight |
| 9 | nine |
| 10 | ten |

## #13 Matching words to colors

On index cards, write the words: red, green, yellow, etc... in red marker. Cut circles or squares of red, green, etc.... Glue them onto index cards. Now make a train with the different colored shapes. Say to your child, "This says red. Find the red shape." Continue until all colors are matched.

# #14 Matching words to animals

Children like to play zoo or farm. Many children like to collect small plastic animals. Whether your child has three or 10 animals, a make-believe farm or zoo, all the animals can be labeled with flash cards. At first your child will need some help. Eventually he will succeed in matching all the animals with the words. When you visit a real zoo, your child will be very excited to read the words on the signs with your help.

# #15 Matching words to continents

Purchase picture flash cards of continents and countries. A map attached to a cork board would also be helpful. Make flash cards for each country and continent. Match words to their country or continent.

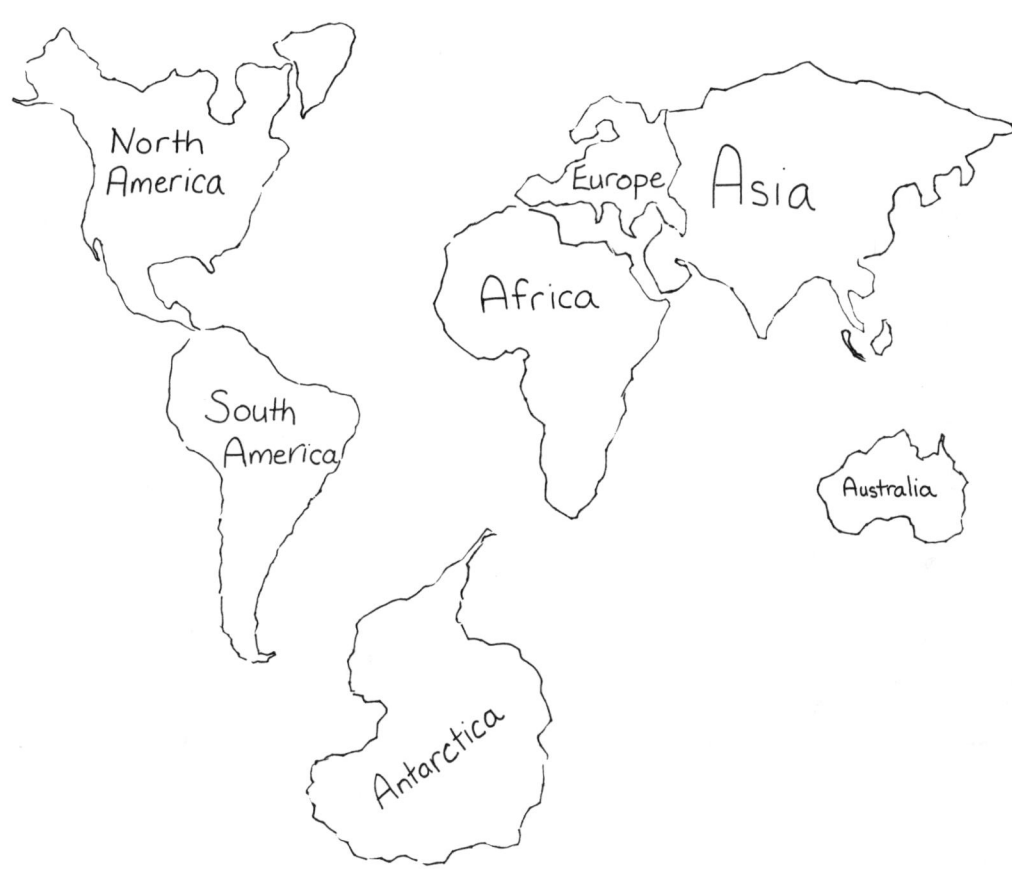

#16  Matching words to states

Purchase flash cards of the 50 U.S. states. Write out the names of the states on index cards. Have your child match the words to the picture flashcards. It would be wise to begin with 10 states, then continue with 20, then 25, etc....

# #17 U.S. puzzle/map

You will need a large U.S. puzzle and a map. Guide your child to construct the outside part of the puzzle which will include the four corners, oceans, Alaska and Hawaii. Have your child begin putting the puzzle together with the western states. They are bigger and easier to locate. With a pencil, point to the state of Washington on the map and read its name. Ask your child to find the Washington state puzzle piece and put it into the correct place in the puzzle. Continue with Oregon, California, Nevada and so on. With young children, it is advisable to complete half of the puzzle in one sitting and continue the next day. Children may want to rush ahead, fitting the pieces of the puzzle together without reading them. Remember that the main goals of this activity are reading and geography. Read each piece or state and indicate its location, e.g. Washington. South of Washington is Oregon, then California. The idea is not to do a puzzle, but rather to locate each state and read the names.

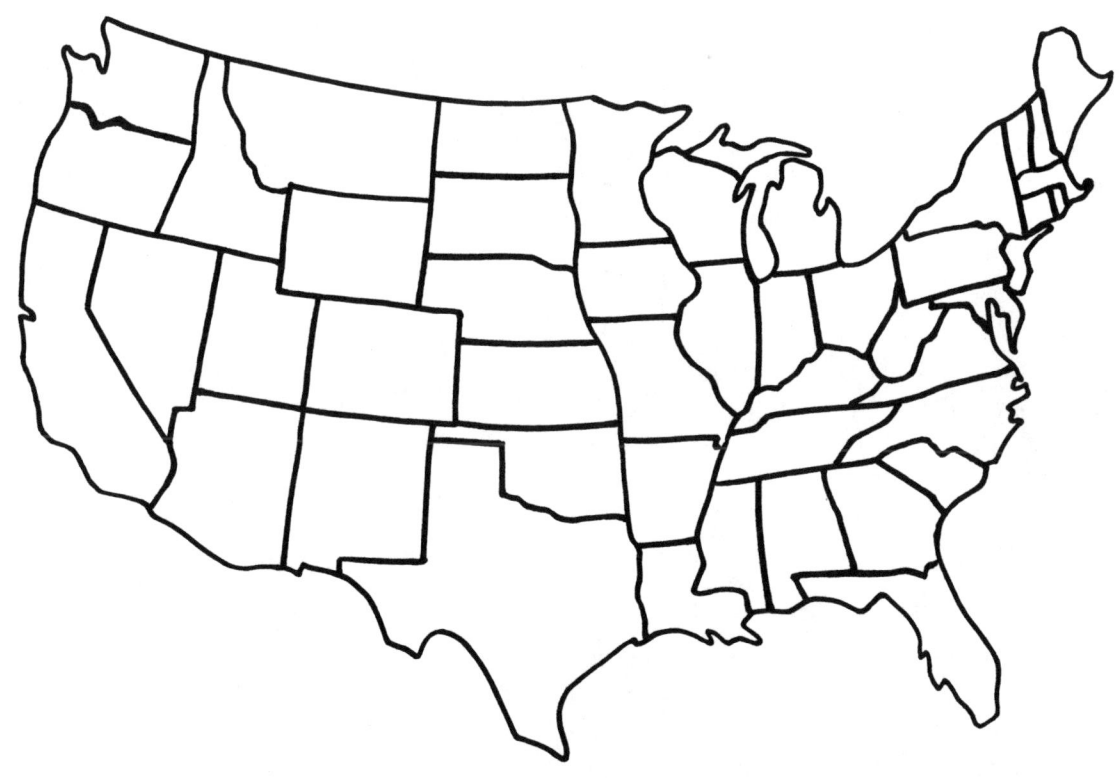

# #18 Finding countries in each continent

You will need maps of the seven continents (a map of Africa, a map of Asia, etc) and flash cards of individual countries. Give your child the map of Europe. Pick up the European country flashcards. Show your child the picture of France and name the country. Ask your child to locate France on the map of Europe. Do the same for Germany, Switzerland, etc.... As he does this activity, point out the shape of each country. This will help your child locate it. Look at the shape. Look at the color.

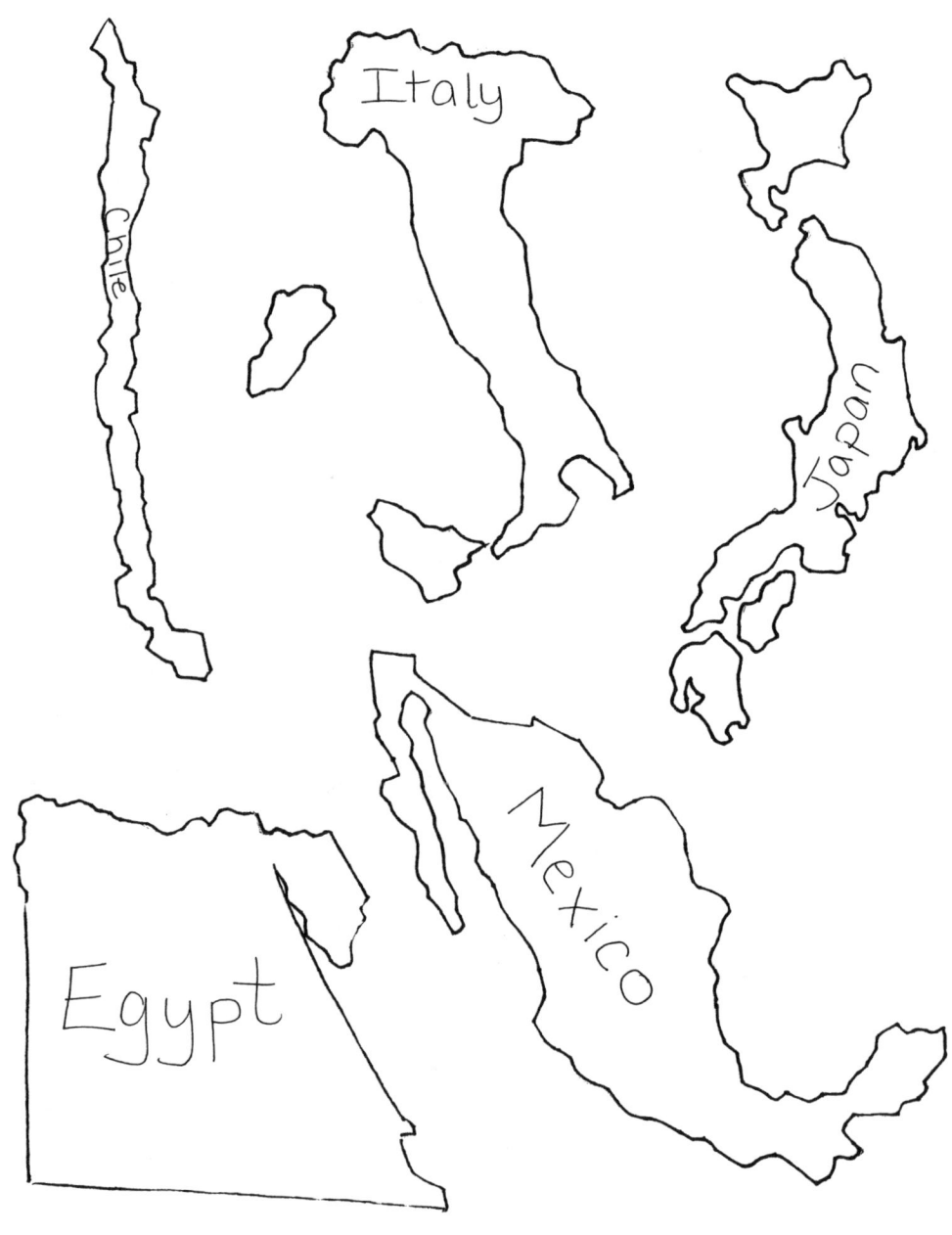

# #19 The globe

A globe is a must. Very young children will see the obvious contrast between water and land and begin to ask questions. The globe is a great tool for reading as well as understanding the earth. Read the names of the continents. Locate our continent, North America. Tell your child that we live in the United States. Finding the state in which he lives will be a fascinating discovery and a lesson in geography.

#20 The Solar System

Buy a large map of the solar system showing the sun and all the planets. Where is the earth? What are the names of the other planets? Simply read them and observe the interest that it will generate.

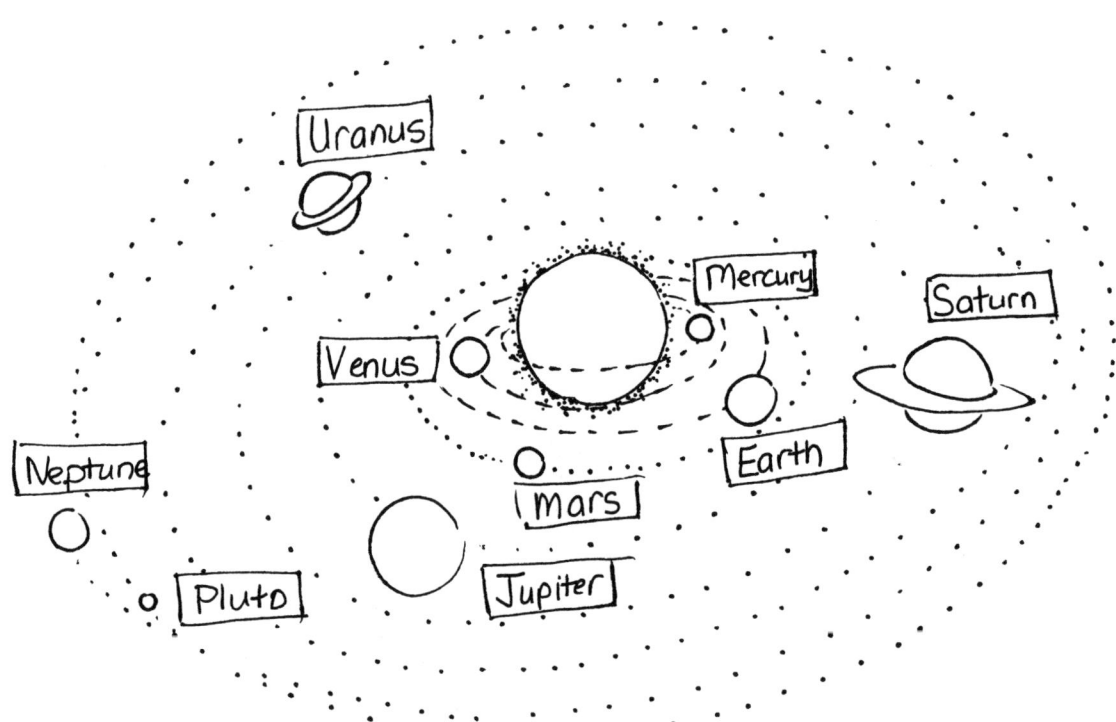

# #21 Opposites

After your child has mastered all 100 sight words and 320 phonics words, he is ready for a new, more challenging way of matching. You will create flash cards in two colors, red and black. One set will be displayed on the table in the form of a train. The other will be given to your child. You will say, "This is whisper. The opposite is...." Wait for the answer.

| | |
|---|---|
| young | old |
| cloudy | sunny |
| smile | frown |
| laugh | cry |
| scared | brave |
| friend | enemy |
| forget | remember |
| whisper | shout |
| question | answer |

# #22 Poetry

The public library will provide an abundance of poetry and nursery rhymes for young children. Simple poetry and rhymes should be included in your reading repertoire. Begin with a simple poem, a few lines long.

Rain, rain go away...come again...some other day.

Your child will memorize poems easily. Read part of each line

>Rain, rain
>come again
>some

and let your child fill in the blanks. You will soon see, perhaps after the third time, that your child can recite the whole poem. Eventually your child will have his own books. He can then read his favorite verses.

Older children can be introduced to more advanced ideas in poetry. The following is a poem I wrote while in college. It shows a change in "mood" and lots of imagery.

## ON THE SEASHORE

There is silence on the shore tonight,
on the rocky salty shore,
the grey, wet shore.
The silent silver little waves
slowly moving on the shore,
whispering a melodious tune,
leaping on the sand,
are not moaning for their task.
All is calm.

The long laborious day is gone,
the ships coming by the port,
the seaman humming a happy tune
returns home bringing the darting, lively fishes
imprisoned by the net caught on the high sea.

The family around the table
enjoying the cooked, fresh, odorous fish.
The seaman tells his tales,
of dangers he encountered on the great immense sea.
Oh! proud, cruel, revengeful sea!
You are robust, powerful, forceful,
yet generous, beautiful, charming!
The seaman bows before your majesty.

But there is silence on the sea tonight;
it is dark! Children dream adventures
of the high sea,
but no one is on the port,
no one is on the sea.

Only on the shore, the music
of the waves, the fresh crystal waves
seem to be humming a very special tune.
What are the waves whispering?
Two hearts are beating,
stars are watching,
the universe listening,
the sky observing
the changes of the sea.

Oh! gigantic, enchanting sea!
you fold upon yourself,
you change your mood,
from grey to green to blue
or from serene to calm, to stormy.
You are limpid, clear and fresh,
and your fragrance touches me!

It touches the silence of this night,
the senses of two hearts. It reaches me!
If you could speak, oh sea, the mysteries
unfolding would be clear to me!
But no! There is deep silence on the shore tonight.

# #23 Songs:

Children enjoy singing. Select simple and well known songs. Twinkle, Twinkle Little Star, It's a Small World, and popular Christmas songs would be good choices. Point to the words with a pencil and sing together. Make sure that your child doesn't sing faster than your pencil moves.

# It's a small world

It's a world of laughter,
a world of tears,
it's a world of hopes,
and a world of fears,
there's so much that we share,
that it's time we're aware,
it's a small world after all.

> It's a small world after all,
> it's a small world after all,
> it's a small world after all,
> it's a small, small world.

There is just one moon,
and one golden sun,
and a smile means friendship to everyone.
Though the mountains divide,
and the oceans are wide,
it's a small world after all.

After you and your child have enjoyed singing together several times and he has learned most of the words, allow him to fill in the blanks. Stop before the end of the sentence and let him finish.

> It's a world of ..........
> a world of......
> it's a world of .....
> and a world of .....
> there's so much that .....
> that it's time we're .......
> it's a small world ......

# #24 Play store

Cut out names of stores from the newspaper. Also cut out words for different items: food, clothing, etc....Display the names of the stores in a semicircle. Line up words for food and clothing under an appropriate store. Pretend to go shopping. Say, "I need some milk. Buy me some." Your child will hand you the word for milk. Continue with other food and clothing items.

| Meat Market | Clothing Store | Pet Shop | Fruits & Vegetables |
|---|---|---|---|
| milk | dress | hamster | broccoli |
| eggs | pants | fish | orange |
| butter | socks | snake | grapes |
| bread | coat | dog | tomato |
| chicken | shoes | cat | strawberries |
| steak | blouse | bird | spinach |
| fish | shirt | lizard | cabbage |
| cake | tie | mice | potato |
| jelly | hat | monkey | lemon |
| lobster | pajamas | rabbit | onions |

# #25 Let's go shopping

Print your shopping list clearly. Leave it on the refrigerator. At the store, give it to your child and have him help you find the items. While shopping, read signs and labels as much as possible.

# #26 Electric board

It's a 24" x 53" structure designed to amuse a child. Ambitious parents will find this project a rewarding experience. We have used it for simple words, street signs, pictures, and names of famous Americans, as well as to give "instant" success. When the answer is correct the light bulb will light up.

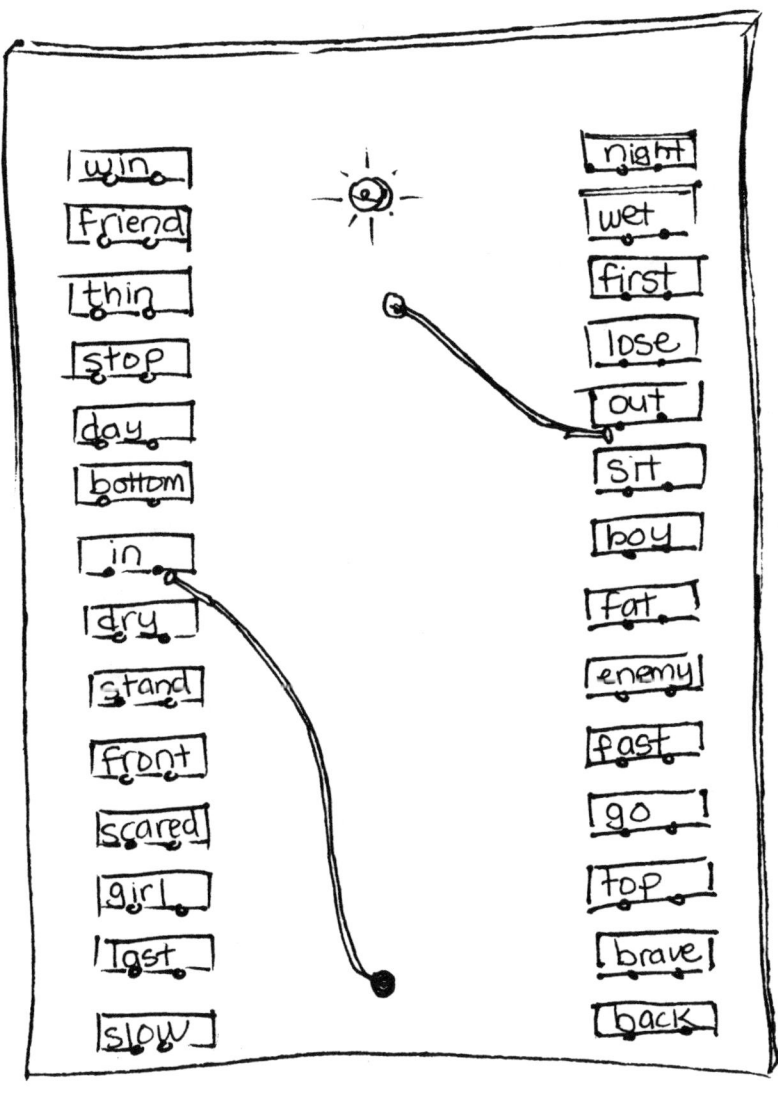

# #27 Making sentences from known words

Simple sentences are one way to introduce words such as: the, in, on, if, my, to, and, etc.... These words out of context have no meaning; worse yet, they cannot be visualized. Children who are given a list of these words are bored out of their minds. No wonder many children "hate" reading! Select those words your child has learned. Introduce him to sentences immediately, perhaps the day after he has mastered his first 5 words. Here are some examples of sentences to use:

**I love my mommy.**

**I love my daddy.**

**I love my sister.**

**I love my brother.**

**I love my family.**

**I love ice cream.**

**I love lemon on fish.**

**I like bread and butter.**

**I like cake and milk.**

# #28 All 'b' words

Children confuse the letters b, d, and p. This activity will focus on the letter 'b'. You have a set of 100 words in your hands. Each word has a different beginning letter. Pull out the word "boy." Say, "This is a 'b' word. Now I am going to flash the cards. When you see a 'b' word, say 'b.'" He may see 'b' when he sees the word "dog." Say, "Whoops! This is a 'd' word." Then continue until you have flashed all 100 words.

#29 Making Stacks
Print the entire alphabet.

| a b c d e f g h i j k l m n o p q r s t u v w x y z |

Have your child make a stack of all the 'a' words under the letter a. Do the same for each letter.

      a             b             c

| apple | boy | carrot |

# #30 Beginning sound

On a large sheet of paper, make a list of your child's favorite 'b' words. Let him read it. Do the same with other letters. Create one page for each beginning sound.

Example:   boy         carrot        dog         tomato
           butter      candy         daddy       table
           brother

The beginning letter should be printed in red so children will see it clearly. Some children have the tendency to reverse the beginning sound and the ending sound. They start at the right rather than the left. This activity will eliminate confusion. Once the 'b' letter and sound are established, the 'd' will be simple. Tell your child that the 'b' is a line and a circle. Have him pretend to make a 'b' with his finger on the table. Tell him then, that the 'd' is a circle and a line.

Oral exercises are another way to reinforce the 'b' sound: I say, "Give me a 'b' word," and my student will say, " boy, butter, etc..." Count how many words he can think of. This activity can be done in the car as well. Where there are two children, write the words.
Example:

| Mark | John |
|------|------|
| boy  | butter |
| baby | brother |

In a classroom setting, the teacher can write the words on the board. Better yet, form teams.

| Team A | Team B |
|--------|--------|
| boy    | butter |
| baby   | brother |

#31 Silly b words

Since the letter "b" is confusing to a young reader why not anticipate and correct the problem before it even begins? This silly story will focus on the "b" sound and show your child "b" words. Have your child trace all the 'b's' with a red magic marker. If the "b" problem continues, a clown with a big stomach will show your child that a "b" is a line and a circle. The circle is to the right. Eventually a student will see the difference between the letters b, d, and p.

I was a baby boy. Now I am a big boy.

My baby brother has a big bat.

He has a bag of baby beans.

He likes to blow big soap bubbles.

b  d  p

b

#32 Body parts

Have your child lie down on the floor. Take parts of the body words -ear, eye, finger, hair, hand, head, heart, stomach, toes, etc, and label the parts of his body. Cover him with these words one by one after flashing the words.

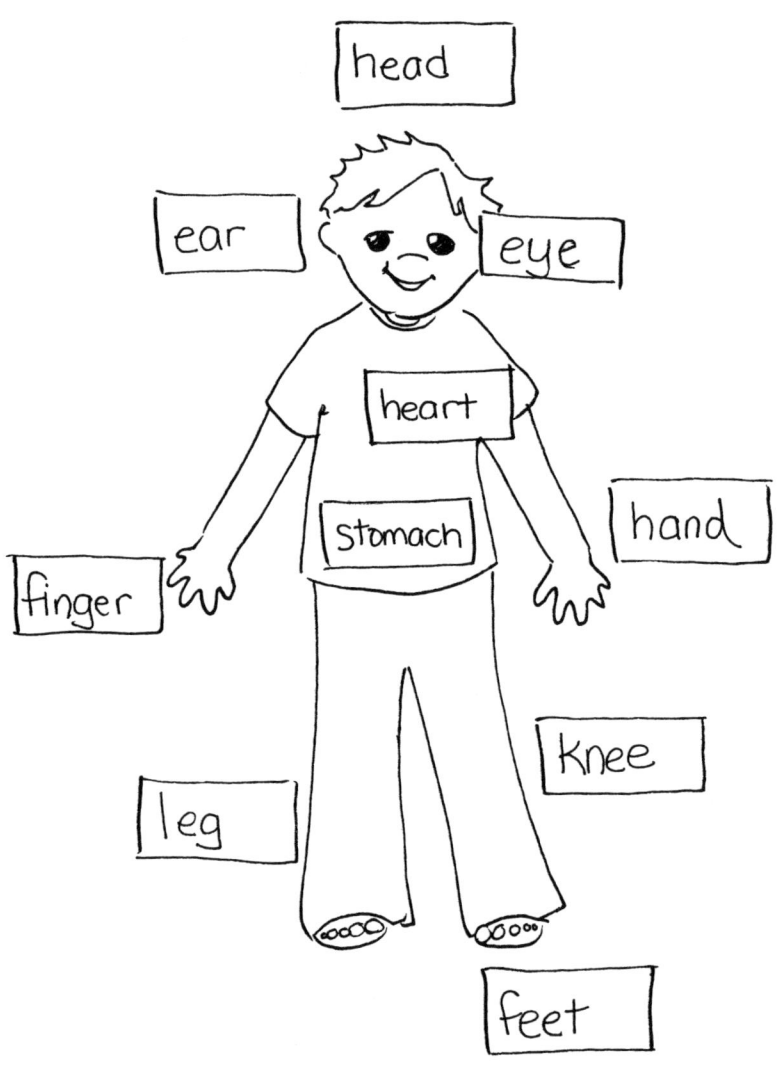

#33 Label furniture and objects around the house.

Words such as closet, door, table, etc. can be attached to their corresponding objects to indicate that everything has a name. Give your child each word, walk around the house and label things. Your child will not miss the opportunity to read these words all by himself. After a few days, remove these words and have him label things without your help. Always rescue him before he makes a mistake.

# #34 Pin words on a cork board

Some words can be pinned on a cork board if your child enjoys seeing them up. He can draw pictures representing these words.

Begin with a small cork board. If it becomes a major attraction, a larger one can be purchased. It will accommodate space for words, pictures, maps, etc. In our house, we had a strong need for more and more space. One entire wall was covered with cork.

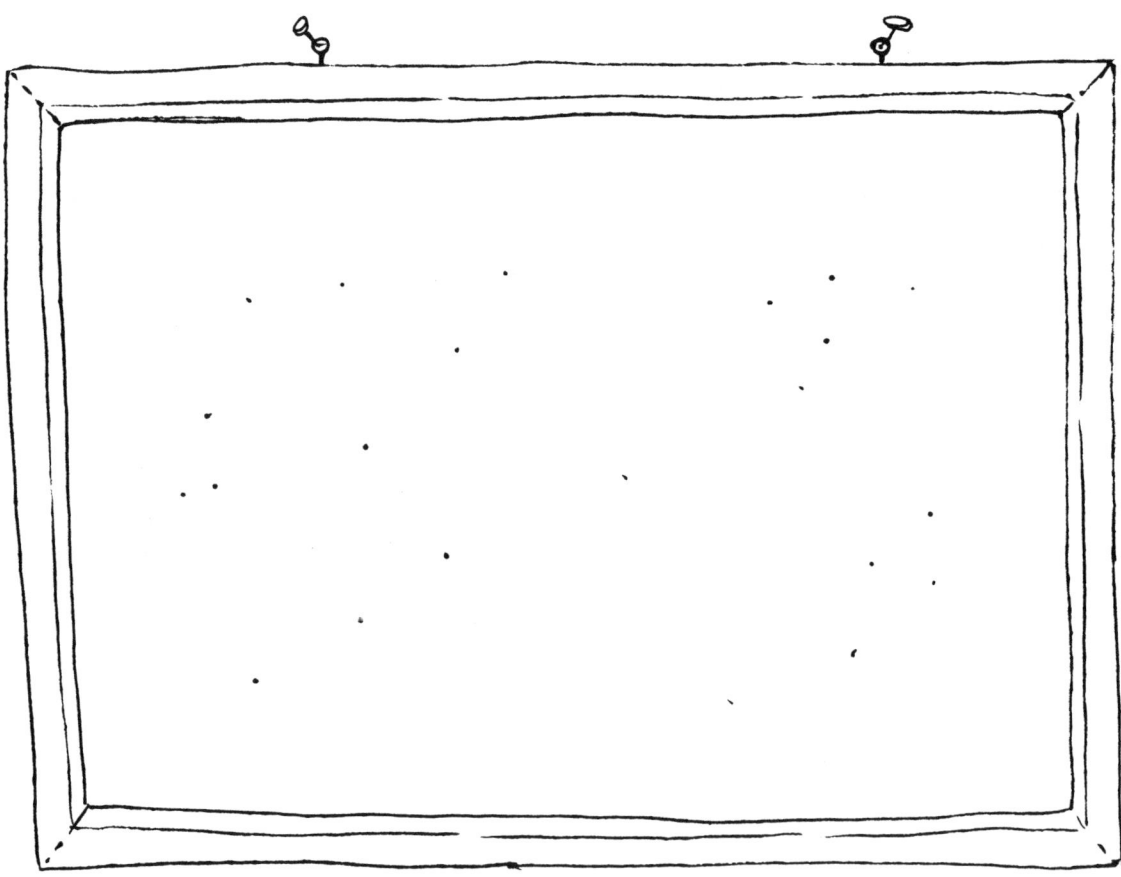

Remember: Always praise your child's art work no matter how unrealistic it appears to you.

## #35 Point to calendar

Before or after breakfast, look at a calendar to promote the reading of months and days. If possible, pin a large calendar on the wall in the kitchen close to the table where breakfast is served.

## #36 Names of Family Members
Pin pictures of family members and their names on the cork board. Most important are the child's picture and name.

# #37 Names of famous people

Pictures of famous people are easy to find and purchase. They can be pinned on the cork board. Some names children should be able to identify are: Abraham Lincoln, George Washington, Sally Ride, Eleanor Roosevelt, Martin Luther King, Jr. Include pictures of scientists, artists, discoverers, architects, etc...It would be wise to be one step ahead of your child. Be prepared to make one statement about each person e.g. George Washington was our first president.

#38  Breakfast time

Breakfast time could be a time to label things on the table. Milk, bread, butter, jelly, sugar, cup, plate, dish, eggs, etc. It is not necessarily a time to "teach" reading, but rather a routine your child will become accustomed to.

#39 Grocery list on the refrigerator

Take a large piece of paper with lines and leave it on the refrigerator. Make a list of all the items you need from the grocery store. Make sure to print the words clearly. Let the list grow. Tell your child what you're doing, preparing this list so next time you and he go to the store you will remember to buy: milk, bread, carrots, oranges etc. Always share with your child what you're doing, thinking, planning, etc.

# #40 Restaurant: paper napkin

You're looking at a menu and your child is hungry and eager to eat. Show him the many choices; point to words and let him select. If he has a choice between several types of food on the menu, you can take the opportunity to point to his choices. There is nothing to do while you wait for the food to be served? Think again. All you need is pen and paper. Write food words on the napkin; challenge your child to make pictures for them. Or ask him to draw a picture and you'll provide the word for it.

# #41 Pencil and paper

Never leave the house without a book as well as pencil and paper. Children as young as two or three love to scribble. Ask your child to scribble something. You then change it to a fish, a house, a boat etc. To make it more interesting, write words next to each picture. Waiting in line somewhere can be turned into a pleasant experience. The important thing is to utilize precious time doing something productive.

# #42 Circles and lines in a story

Your child can now read most of the 320 phonics words and 100 sight words. He has been introduced to simple sentences and songs. Now is the time for him to read paragraphs as well as simple stories. Your child will read successfully by following these steps:

1. Read the whole paragraph or 2-3 pages if you choose a simple book.
2. Ask your child to read for you.
3. As he reads he will pause on words he is not familiar with.
4. When he pauses immediately provide the word for him. Underline or circle in pencil the words he cannot read.
5. Allow your child to read the paragraph or pages a second time.
6. As he reads you will notice that words he could not read the first time are now clear to him. When he reads the word with confidence, erase the line or the circle.
7. At the end your child will see that all circles and lines have been removed and he will have experienced success. Reward these first steps by attaching a sticker on each "perfect" page.

# #43 Select and print sight words from a story

Readability, the ability to read, must "grow." You want your child to read anything. To this end, you will choose the next level of difficulty in reading. Readability is not to be confused with comprehension. A child must read first, then comprehend. This book, however, does not deal with comprehension.

Select a story that is both inspiring and teaches a specific value. Read the story with enthusiasm, appropriate intonation and feeling. Read clearly. Discuss the characters, the setting, etc.... Go back to paragraph one. Read it clearly, then ask your child to read for you. Those words he cannot read should be transferred onto cards. Continue the process for several paragraphs or pages. Now you have 10-20 flash cards. Flash quickly. Continue until all pages in the book have been read and all cards have been printed. Flash them every day. Go back to the beginning, read clearly, then have your child read to you. Tell him, "Words you don't know we will underline." As he reads, quickly provide words he cannot read. If you own the book, underline them in pencil. It would be a mistake to make your child struggle. Ask your child to read the first underlined word. If he cannot, quickly read it for him. If he reads it correctly, erase the line. When you have erased all the lines, move on to the next page. Ask your child to read each page "perfectly" then proceed to the next. You can put a sticker onto the pages your child reads with confidence.

Eventually, it will be unnecessary to transfer words onto cards. It will be sufficient to provide the word once and your child will remember. Down the road, dictionary skills will have to be taught, for even a parent will not be familiar with the pronunciation of certain words.

## #44 Find a treat

When your child can read short sentences, reward him with a surprise, a treat to be found. Announce that you have a surprise for him. Give him a note that says, for example:

---

Go to the table. Look under the plate.

---

Under the plate he will find another note. It will say

---

Now look under your small red chair.

---

Under the plate he will find another note. It will say

---

Please walk up the stairs, go to your bedroom and look under your pillow.

---

Under the plate he will find another note. It will say

---

Walk to the closet; give your mommy a big hug. Say, "I love you, Mommy." Now walk to the closet, open it, and look for a red package. Open it, then say, "Thank you, Mommy."

Write these notes according to your child's desires and his ability to read. Here are some examples of what I did with my students and children. This time my goal was to reinforce these words: germ, vaccine, invisible, surprise, etc....

# Clue #1

I want you to know that you're very important to me.
I realize that you don't have the Louis Pasteur book. Still you can read words like: **germs** and **vaccine**. Look under a big sea shell.

# Clue #2

Don't worry. Your surprise is not invisible because it is something you really want. Look under your chart.

# Clue #3

Hurry, I promised something that is sure to make you laugh. You have to believe me. Go toward my desk; next to it there is a big chair. What's on it? Look inside.

Another example:

# Clue #1

> What a year this has been! I would say, "Well done." Your parents have decided that you're comfortable when you read- Look around the phonics game.

# Clue #2

> Since your reading is almost magical, I promised to let you find another surprise. Look under your chart.

# Clue #3

> Enough is enough. If you don't want an invisible surprise, go near the set of red books close to the floor.

Giving notes with clues became a tradition in our family. When something special was to be given, it was always done with notes. This time, we had purchased a new violin for one of our girls.

# Clue #1

There is a surprise just waiting to be found. It's hidden somewhere, but not underground. Before you may have this wonderful thing, you have to guess what it might be. Think!
Look in the money drawer!

# Clue #2

It is not wrapped. It would cost too much. But wait until you see it. It will feel good to your touch.
Look under the coffee maker.

# Clue #3

It will make many trips to and from the usual place. We must be careful with it, too hot or too cold temperatures will damage its face.
Look under your pillow.

# Clue #4

It gives your mom pleasure. It puts your dad to sleep. Your sister couldn't care less. She goes back to her mess.
Look in the cabinet. See glasses.

## Clue #5

It is long. It is thin. It has something that rhymes with row. Some people handle it right. It brings joy to one's ears. But if done wrong, it might bring tears.
Look under the hamper.

## Clue #6

Many teachers appreciate it, but one in particular will look at your toes. Your feet are tired, your fingers won't move, but that's how it goes.
Look in Shawn's violin case.

## Clue #7

Well, you get the idea, but it's not the right size. Go into Mom's closet for your big surprise. Bring it down and let us hear. Is this thing really so dear?

Excitement built until my daughter found her violin, yelling and screaming thank-yous. We still have that on video tape.

Another example:

---

1. Are you eager to find a surprise? Then go immediately! Look under a little purple rug near the phonics game.

---

2. It is dreadful not to find your surprise in this department. You have to concentrate more. Go under the Solar system game.

---

3. This is terrible! You need more information and you will certainly find it. Go look under a red chair.

---

Sometimes my students would receive clues in a simple letter.

---

Dear Kassandra,
    Do you like to read? Are you precious to your mom and dad? Does your grandpa love you? Does your grandma love you? Circle one.

    YES                                                   NO

Now look under the table. You will find a nice surprise. Now give your teacher a big hug because your teacher loves you.

## #45. Egg hunt - write notes - give clue

On Easter, we would hide eggs and candy. We gave the egg hunt a different twist by writing notes.

Use your legs to find the eggs.
If you use the following clues,
you'll see the prize before your eyes.

Now, you'll find some socks in a big red box,
if you want some fun, try to choose the right one.

In that one you'll see an egg as pretty as can be.
Then you can take it. Be careful don't break it.

And also there you'll find a note.
Read it well, so you can tell.

There's another egg in a toy boat.
In this boat you will see an egg and
a note saying go to a tree..


More clues:

Tree: run like a fox
      to check the mail box

Mail box: run to the big rocks
      but don't lose your socks.
      Now choose the one of the biggest size
      and there it will be before your eyes

Rock: Look, it makes sense, to go to the fence,
      and look under the gate but don't be late.

Gate: You don't have to go far to find a big jar.

Jar: If to the west you stare, you'll spot a white chair

Chair: The next egg will be in the branch of a tree.

# #46. Parents reading to children

Reading to children is a pleasure reserved mostly for parents. It begins very early and continues until a child becomes a totally independent reader. Occasionally when you read, you see how many words your child can find on a particular page. Before attempting this strategy, make sure the page has words he knows. Say to him, "I bet you can find a word you know on this page." This activity is appropriate only after your child has successfully read half of all the sight words and phonics.

Remember: always set your child up for success

## #47. Make up stories

Purchase a notebook. On one side of the page attach photos of your child, family members and activities. On the opposite side tell about the photos. The sentences should be simple and printed in large letters.

| | |
|---|---|
| Page 1 | I am a baby boy (girl).<br>My name is ..... |
| Page 2 | This is my mommy.<br>I love my mommy. |
| Page 3 | This is my daddy.<br>I love my daddy. |
| Page 4 | This is my brother (name).<br>and my sister (name).<br>I love my brother.<br>I love my sister. |

Include pictures of special events such as birthdays.

| | |
|---|---|
| Page 5 | I am 1 year old.<br>This is my cake.<br>I love cake. |

When your child begins to read, he will enjoy seeing words about himself. Reading the words you have written about him will make him feel loved.

#48. Action words

On index cards print action words: running, drinking, crying, jumping, sleeping, etc. Flash each one, then ask your child to pretend to do what the card says. If he hesitates to read the word, provide the answer for him immediately. The second time he may be able to play this game without your help.

#49. Books on shelves

Children are often able to select their favorite books by the pictures on the cover. Some books, however, can be identified only by the title. When you read to your child make sure to point out the words on the book cover. Make it a habit to send him to his collection to pick up books. Follow him and help him if he needs it.

## #50. Notes in the lunch box

Small children often feel homesick when they first go to school. From the very beginning it will be comforting to your child to find a love note in the lunch box. A simple note that says:

> I love you

followed by a hand drawn heart - will surely give your child the message that he is not alone. Eventually your child will be able to read more lengthy notes. These should be appropriate to his ability to read. Example:

> This peanut butter is good for you. Eat your orange, drink all your milk. I love you.

Now that you have explored these pages, let me congratulate you. You probably already have in your possession our kits that will give your child/students the power to read. Remember you will need a phonics program.

# Play & Read

## Matching.............
## Making.............
## Reading........
## Spelling......

It contains: 1 Student's Progress Chart, 1 Instruction Booklet, 1 Video, 20 Boards 24" X 17", 320 Flash Cards, 6" X 4", and over 1,400 letters 2" X 2".

Remember: You also need a whole language program. This kit has 100 words in red and 100 words in blue. There are also 20 color pictures.

# Play & Read

# Sight Words Kit

Remember: A young child needs easy reading in a story form. Large words are one important element. The Spoons on the Moon and A Snail in the Pail reenforce the phonics sounds learned in the Play & Read kit (phonics). To give you an idea, the first two pages are reproduced here.

A snail
 in a
 pail

Once upon a time
 there was a snail in a pail
How did this happen?

A sailor was sailing on the sea when he saw a poor baby snail making a trail on a rail on a sail on the sea.

In these books, the phonics component (in this case ail) is in red. You will see that each book (20 in all) utilizes all 16 words on a board. These little "people" spoons and snails have a conflict that is resolved by going home to mama and papa. The bright colors of the pictures and the story itself will capture your child's/children's imagination.

Dear parents, friends, educators,

Welcome to Lifelong Learning Systems, a family oriented company dedicated to the educational success of our children. And now that you have given me the privilege of entering your home/classroom, I would love to hear from you. Won't you write or call to tell me your stories? In the meantime, happy reading and best wishes for a warm and rewarding relationship with your child/children.


Nancy Goldhagen
Author


Seminars are available. To register call:

Lifelong Learning Systems, Inc.<br>
630-773-2363<br>
e-mail: lifelong9@aol.com

Tutoring/classes are offered on many levels. We welcome the very young in a Play & Read program (limit 4 per class).

Finally, to allow a child to practice writing, you can purchase workbooks. <u>A Snail in the Pail</u> workbook version is an example. Your child will color the picture and do the writing on the opposite side.

Lifelong Learning Systems, Inc.

Order Form

Name:_____

Address:_____

City/State/Zip:_____

Phone_____

E-mail_____

| Quantity | Description | Unit Price | Total |
|---|---|---|---|
|  |  |  |  |

| | |
|---|---|
| Subtotal | |
| Sales Tax | |
| Shipping | |
| Total | |